# FINNEGAN UNBOUND

# FINNEGAN UNBOUND

by

David Krause



THE DOLMEN PRESS

Set in Palatino type by Redsetter Ltd. and
printed in Ireland for

The Dolmen Press
Mountrath, Portlaoise, Ireland

Designed by Liam Miller

First published 1986

ISBN 0-85105-438-2 The Dolmen Press

For the Ireland
that made me
and Jack Paris
who also helped

CONTENTS

# I

## FINNEGAN'S CAUL

Safely cauled in his mother's sea
He floated symbiotically

Suspended like a coddled egg
Fermenting in a honey keg

Away and awash in spicy froth
He saw the world through seaweed cloth

Preserved it as his talisman
A relic for a drifting man
Who hoped to die abed amen

## JUICE

No I cannot improvise it
Mock it up with scissors and paste

I need red nerves to mount my skit
I have to see and feel and taste
The bit of bone that held the hair
The compost clay that fed the worms

I dread the fox that bled the hare
But kiss the wound the fire burns
There is no juice without the germs

## STAR DANCE

When the choreography of stars
Strikes blue flame from earth-bound stones
Leap for the liquid taste of air
Or inhale the worm-dust of bones

Will you waltz madame or hoard crumbs
Is the act gracehoppers or ants

When the fire spears beat their drums
Will you ape moles or elephants

Diggers to dross and dancers dance

## SWEET LION

Heroes must be doom-eager
Yeats read it in an epic story
About the druidic daimonizer
That goads men to blood glory

Cuchulain and Connolly and Pearse

There's more vital blood for seeds of verse
In the sacrifice of Sheehy-Skeffington
Sweet lion of peace who lost and won
The crown of love-eager simpleton

## PREYING

Will the cock lose his tread
With the hen if a hawk
Hides at her nesting bed

Will the stricken brood balk
To break free of the shell
With a masked falcon head

Were the cauldrons of hell
Bubbling under the hearth
Where God brewed Adam's birth

## DJH

I hold his daimon in my heart
It goads me and I nurture it

But when I try to play his part
I mime his holy idiot

His consciousness makes such a noise
I tremble when I share his toys

He was my martyr from the start
His icon now burns in my blood
Since I may fall where he once stood

## MENANDER'S CRATO

If by chance some god enticed me

"Crato, after you die you'll rise
Again in any new shape free
To choose whatever I devise
A cat a cow a pig a sheep
A dog a goat a horse a man"

I'd entreat him to let me sleep
Deep in my grave unless he can
Make me anything but human

## SPIDERLUST

There is a spider in my mind
Who spins a web of infant stars

His entrails elevate and bind
The quest for my lost avatars

He weaves what I confide in sleep
My secrets have no other voice

I scale his samarkand to keep
His bargain to redeem my choice

I have the bowels for paradise

## MONET

Eyeless in Giverny he saw
Totemic poplars quivering
Like mauve ladies flushed in awe
Of water lilies offering
Their petals green blood-red and white

Luscious pads of laughter floating
Oh lilies lilies burnt in light

From an angel's cradle doting
On the brash titan's ravished sight

## CARRION HEART

The sparrow of my innocence
Abstained from worms to fast and pray

My hawk now screams for recompense
To scourge those callow years away

I cannot hide as I did then
My talons ache now and conspire

If by chance I could live again
In a rose nest or a black pyre
My carrion heart would eat fire

## ANGEL SWEAT

Raddle my loins with reddest dye
I seized a blessed damozel
And risked damnation because I
Copulated with an angel

Covered her wings with mortal clay
That she might carry songs for me
For which she fixed the price I pay

Her labor breaks my slavery
Mere angel sweat delivers me

## INCARNATION
(*for Eileen O'Neill*)

A pear-shaped turquoise Aynsley vase
Anoints this sprig of white heather

A cloistered amulet that was
Only yesterday in tether
On the crest of the Knockmealdowns

And now the cool pine forest dew
On its creamy petals astounds
Our senses which restore the view
In this chalice of where it grew

# II

---

## FINNEGAN'S CLAW

The craft of verse
Is new to me

I make it terse
Astringently

I wring the neck
Of rhetorick

My less is more
Quick salt before
I claw the shore

## RAVEN LOVE

On Creaden Head they cry brook-brook
Black silk among the cuckoo spit
Dive through the clotted snow to hook
Beak and tail in their mating skit

Wheel and glide wing to wing they dip
And roll from cliff to sea and cliff

Against furze and heather they rip
The sky apart and love as if
Their brook-brook could fuse their grip

## SEA TURTLE

Our monster in the salmon net
Was spawned next to eternity

But now his fate is land beset
He flails the leeward enemy

What tidal blunder wrenched his place
What mysteries in his grimace
Would doom us to the ancient flood
Could we dare probe his carapace
To find the twilight face of God

## FELIX FLY

It flew into the sacred cup
And swelled like bread in wine just as
The celebrant had raised it up
To consecrate the morning Mass

Body and blood now in that fly
Had joined the anguished joy of Christ

So priest must drink and fly must die
And since the death was doubly blessed
Insect became the Eucharist

## SANCTUARY

Those snow geese masquerade as swans
They glide through grass like pleasure craft
Arrayed in ranks of haughty clans
With goslings tacking fore and aft

Fearless our endangered species
Cruise and preen as predicated
By their gozzerd's legal mercies

Darwin's claw has abdicated
God and man are vindicated

## FIVE-COLORED PARAKEET

Did the Emperor Hui-tsung see
The same five-colored parakeet
I see perched on that cherry tree
Where four thousand years wink and meet

Does time stand still for him and me
Because art wakes eternally

Do chaste blossoms of yesterday
Burst through that prism on this day
When royal bird serves common clay

## THE THRUSH'S ANVIL

That songbird is a mighty smith
Who smashes snail shells for his meat

His golden throat but half his myth
It makes him strong as he is sweet

Feathers of the meadow flier
Point to his stigmata marker
Sharp anvil stone haloed with briar

He the hammer and the harper
Work and song consume his fire

## CURLEW

A flashing scythe he flits and wheels
To catch the turning of the tides
And harvest ragworms and sandeels

Rife on the churning surf he rides
Crying cur-lew cur-lew cur-lew

His call stakes out his hunting claim
And rakes the strand with foaming rue
When that shrill moan enshrines his name
Crying cur-lew cur-lew cur-lew

## CYGNET FATE

A God begot their princess once
Who toppled towers in the dust

But if their bumpy paddle dance
Now charms no hearts and breaks no trust
There's hubris in their arrogance
That tastes temptation in the crust
Cast on the sea by God not chance

Swans know heaven can be unjust
But cygnets dream of divine lust

## GRAIL OF LIGHT

In the night a slug navigates
Across my floor and leaves a trail
Of silver slime that separates
The first dawn from the last black veil

Thus he bends the heavenly wheels
And as the star of morning grows
I rise to spy a grail that heals

It matters not that no one knows
Where he comes from or where he goes

## THE DAWN CHORUS

Their matin songs define air space
From field to branch to open skies

All birds assert their sacred place
And sweeten first light with sheer cries

The risen larks launched on their dive
Tilt their territorial gong
To warn predators and contrive
Their tread: the weak unlike the strong
Lilt air to measure right from wrong

## PARADISE LOST

(*for the Parises*)

A fool's gold finch that fled its bars
Fluttered antic at our window

Was it searching for seeds or stars
In darkling glass that couldn't show
The mirage would end in hoarfrost

When lust to know is at its peak
The cage of paradise is lost

Did that bird dance to lure the meek
Is death the freedom they all seek

# III

---

## FINNEGAN'S BREAD

Buttered bread always falls
Butter-side-down, they said

It's axiomatic. When Finnegan's
Bread fell butter-side-up again
He sought a ruling from a Franciscan

Who took the enigma to his cell
For meditation until he could tell
His explanation: That piece of bread
Was buttered on the wrong side, he said

## STILL LIFE

The buddhist tale that flowers scream
When plucked is meant to chasten man

Yet God's ripe grace denies that dream
Of pain wrung out of nature's plan

Does the grain groan when reaped for bread
Does the pulled mandrake bleed and shriek

Does the vased tulip lose its head
Does the fresh cut rose stain its cheek

Live buds stay chaste in a new bed

## PERENNIALS

When they died the elegant old ladies
Bequeathed to us their potted plants
To keep them alive like the Pleiades

And now something of their majesty grants
A special dispensation to this house

So we salute the stars in arch repose
Those perennial ladies without regrets
Who designed a memorial that begets
Busy lizzies and African violets

## ABRAHAM

That was not the voice of God
Ordering Abraham to make a choice
Of his son Isaac as sacrifice

No. It was not a divine voice
That measured love by obedience
And pleasured the vanity of a King

In forcing a father to kneel and bring
His oath. What if Abraham broke and railed
Against it. He passed the test God failed

## MY FATHER AGONISTES

If sorrow can dry up the blood
His gritty atoms generate
My love to an electric flood
Of rage that consecrates his fate

Since day by day I die his death
And thus compound the heartbeats when
I share his life with every breath

Such grief can conjure time and then
His hourglass drips blood again

## HARVEST

To press her like an amber grape
And separate the pulp from pips
Can ferment blood when heart agape
I quench my thirst on claret lips

Her vineyard is my harvest shrine
I tread there as her sacristan
And take her wafer with her wine

No sacrilege if mortal man
Can make the profane so divine

## HEAUTON TIMOROUMENOS

Am I the gash am I the knife
Am I the death am I the life

Am I the niagara of love
And hate that immolates the rock
Of faith and cracks the sky above
Until my mirrored monsters mock
The holy blood that might quench thirst

Am I the least am I the first
Am I the beast am I the worst

## SINNERS

I came to you with dragon guilt
Ready to quench fire at your feet
And let my sodden vices wilt
Before your merciful conceit

But you were painting your toenails
Disdainful of my shrove design
Which buckles in a heart that fails

Pain becomes you and I resign
To love you when your sins are mine

## UNICORNS AND GRYPHONS

If unicorns could speak
We would not understand

The language of the meek
Is human contraband

But gryphons might reply
Their fury fits man's roar

Fell beasts would not deny
Their kinship in man's spoor
Blood brothers carnivore

## COPY RITE

Saint Columkille claimed his copy
Of Finnian's Psaltery by right
Of transcription but lost his plea
To own the words that scribes indite
When King Diarmuid read his judgment

"Every cow its calf enfolds
So every book its copy holds"

His halo and his nose now bent
Columkille coughed up copy rent

## SATAN'S MOON

Like women who disdain the worm
When the quarter-moon neaps the tide
The fish refuse to bite on form

That turgid flow denies a ride
To randy seamen high and dry
With lunar penance bought too late

Why fumble with slack lines or try
To tickle trout at heaven's gate
When Satan's moon befouls the bait

## WEXFORD COMMON

The wind that shakes the barley shakes
This Catherine-wheel of tormentil

A golden tapestry that makes
The blushing scarlet pimpernel
Stand guard before these virgin blooms

While briar and furze bracken and fern
Stalk or bristle like proud bridegrooms

Intruders on this scene should learn
That only the faithful dare return

# IV

## FINNEGAN'S SON

Peeping in his da's mystery book
He spied a send-up by Picasso

Three dreamy clowns in a holy show
They were like a picture he once took
When he was in his mummy's tummy

Three creamy kids without a care
We'll dance and hide forever here

The uncle laughed and called him dummy
But he knew his da had put them there

## IMMEMORIAL HOOK
*(for Geoff Cronin)*

Those minted fish fossils took
Root in limestone at the Hook
To proclaim our ancient heritage
Which nothing can obliterate

For when they scuttled out of the sea
That mothered them and sanctioned
This peninsula as their sacristy
They sculpted our graven selves that time
Forever in the immemorial slime

## GENTLE WRAITH

Part of me died when my mother died

Part of me went with her into the hallowed
Ground and remained there when I tried
To intercede with the shade that followed
Her into the unfathomed bed of eternity

I commiserated with her gentle wraith
Because that part of me refused liberty
From the umbilical shroud that binds our faith

Now we know part of me lives in her death

## ELEGY FOR DONAL 1
*(for Kathleen Gough)*

They told me you were dead but we
Know a floating man only sleeps
In clouds upon that Wexford sea

He links his dreamy salmon leaps
To rainbow suns that split the sky
With God's ripe rain at Dollar Bay

You hover there where seabirds cry
And new waves wash old shells away
Your sea-change makes death die each day

## ELEGY FOR DONAL 2

If I should die before you wake
I'll look for you where dolphins play
Off Hook Head rocks where rain waves rake
The salt of life and seed the Bay

If I should live after your sleep
Restores you wholly sanctified
My heart would wrack unless I keep
You floating sapphire at my side
Until death sinks below the tide

## ELEGY FOR DONAL 3

Death only ends if you can live
Again a flasher like Hook Light

Since grief has no more tears to give
Your beacon cleaves my darkest night

From this day every mortal knows
You float there like a glory child
Through sweet sea gates that never close

A dove wheeled on a wave beguiled
When death and I were reconciled

## LEX TALIONIS

Salt shrunk shark jaws
Pumiced to stone

Sea liced crab claws
Of toothless bone

God's messages
For transient man

Who ravages
With taloned hand
The holy strand

## SLADE CASTLE

Those cormorants gave death a ride
Into the hunt like a knife blade
Sweeping the sea with ravished pride
As black beaks plundered prey off Slade

We should have known they etched a sign
Of unappeased blood wrung through stone
By a god thirsty and malign

Do we all go those shoals alone
where furies strip us to the bone

## BALLYGUNNER CHURCHYARD
*(for the Goughs and Tilsons and Cronins)*

There is no sweeter place to sleep
Where Celtic crosses and tall weeds
Like icons of the untilled earth keep
Watch over the immortal seeds
Of sons of fathers lost and found

The bones that lie here live again
And generate the sainted ground

They hold our store of foretold grain
While we kneel singing in our pain

## MAYFLY DANCE

Behind Slade Castle at high tide
The mackerel join the mayfly dance

United in their foamy ride
Blood strikes them in their mated trance

Men, women and boys on the rocks
Haul in their catch on laden hooks

Fish and fly die ecstatically
Ten thousand years spawned in the sea
Man steals his hour from destiny

## MARCELLA POGORZELSKI
## (1933-1979)

The color of tragedy is red
A scream of bloodflow in the night
That inundates her noble head
Then drains the brainpan of its light

There she lies in serene dumbshow
Redeemed now in her sceptred bed

She knows what we can never know
Since she has overcome the fright
That comedy alone is white

## FROM A DEAD CHILD

My red cross is a bluebird tree
Whose seven branches drape the sky
With silver leaves that shroud a plea
For stricken chicks who bleed and cry

We know the bones of Holocaust
The doomsday wounds of Calvary

If I am dead I am not lost
My yellow star will quicken me
When God redeems my destiny

# V

## FINNEGAN UNBOUND

You scold me for my rush-to-rhyme
And say I need a looser line

Holy Saltmartin where's the crime
If I beat my time incarnadine
Because I can't muck up the sound
And let the sense betray the song

How can I play at hare and hound
If I forget where I belong
I know I'm Finnegan unbound

## SCAVENGER OF LOVE

In the false dawn of sacrilege
A magpie pecking and screeching fed
On snails outside our window ledge

He cried truce to the monkey bed
Where we lay hiding at the edge
Of mortal dreams that could not keep

Us safe from claws until we pledge
Our chastened flesh in the knowledge
That God's scavengers never sleep

## BLUE HORSES

I am no mountain man
Fresh water sickens me

Only ocean salt can
Sweeten my anatomy

A diver not a climber
Submerged and risen free

Reborn to remember
Blue horses bleach the sea
That daily christens me

## SCARECROW OF SILK

Like fuchsia bells licking his face
In a kind wind her silky things
Anointed him with purple grace
An ecstasy of ancient kings

But how could he redeem her price
A laundry hedge his trysting place

Where amulets of sacrifice
Exude her frankincense and myrrh
A heather cairn his masque of her

## FIRST COMMUNION

From Castletown to Tara Hill
The sweetbirds celebrate His will

A drop of chrism on the head
Concocts a caul of gingerbread

They taste their vows when they caress
The angelcake of blessedness

Such rebirth leavens hot advice

Why pray for crumbs like altar mice
God's love is baked with fire not ice

## TOTEM

Outrages that your gargoyle
Daily prompts you to commit
Prove she is the secret foil
Of your sleeping motherwit

Only she can set you free
Save you from a servile fit
Of bowed head and bended knee

Gorge her flesh and gulp her blood
That gipsy totem masks your god

FISHES AND LOAVES
(*for Mardy*)

The fish sleep in parentheses
They trim the gong of water time
And hover in their deep sea trees

Until the tide tells them to climb
And then they whisper as they wake
To face the world of hooks and nets

We fill the loaves for heaven's sake
And sacrifice with no regrets
A fisherman has paid our debts

## DIANA

The sea was there before the land
Rose up to powder into sand

All living things rode on the foam
Out of the womb that was our home

A virgin moon conceived the waves
That washed us out of warm sea caves

If mother sea needs father land
It takes a bride to make a strand
And hold the ocean in her hand

## WINKLE PARABLE

A conch adrift on the shore's crust
Tornadoed by the August tide
Betrays a trail of winkle dust

On quickened sand he must ride
Back to his maternal foam
Before the terns make meat of him

How can I find my long way home
When torrents rend me heart from limb
Until I rather drift than swim

## TINKER GIRL IN GORT

In the Lady Gregory country
I was transfixed by a remote
Girl who froze the brute blood in me

Why did the wake of wild goat
Drench all her bronze beauty

What was the bite if the antidote
Missed the dung in her pot of honey

Even when my fears have ceased
Do they presume beauty is the beast

# THE SEA'S ECONOMY

The sea's economy is just
All who eat or are eaten grow
Again as fin or claw and must
Ravage life to restore its flow
Without residue or decay

There's no starvation and no sin
Those crimes that only men display

The dust crushed land where death-heads grin
The bell sprung sea where dreams begin

## SEA CHANGE
(*for Anne*)

September seas baptize the flesh
In ice foam spiced with fired salt

We ride the waves like giddy fish
Who fly all nets and hooks to vault
The sky and plumb the pearly deeps

Dive and rise in a maiden tree
And churn the tide with mandrake leaps

To dance immersed and cauled till we
Burst from the surf changed utterly